Our Favorite
Meatless
recipes

Copyright 2021, Gooseberry Patch
Previously published under ISBN 978-1-62093-009-0

Cover: Laurie's Stuffed Peppers (page 15)

The best thing about the farmers' market...everything is
locally grown, in season. Plump strawberries are ready in June;
blueberries and beans in July; corn, melons and peaches
in August; and apples and pumpkins in October. Enjoy!

Stir-Fried Sesame Vegetables

Serves 4 to 6

1-1/2 c. vegetable broth
3/4 c. long-cooking rice,
    uncooked
1 T. butter
2 T. peanut oil
1/2 lb. asparagus, cut into
    1-inch pieces
1 red pepper, cut into 1-inch
    squares

1 yellow onion, sliced
2 c. sliced mushrooms
2 t. fresh ginger, peeled
    and minced
1 t. garlic, minced
3 T. soy sauce
1 T. sesame oil
1 T. toasted sesame seed

In a saucepan, combine broth, rice and butter. Cover and bring to a boil over high heat. Reduce heat to low; cover and simmer for 15 minutes. Meanwhile, heat peanut oil in a large skillet over medium-high heat. Add vegetables, ginger and garlic; stir-fry for 4 to 5 minutes, or until crisp-tender. Stir in soy sauce and cook for 30 seconds. Remove from heat; stir in sesame oil and sesame seed. Serve over rice.

Look for all kinds of delicious, nutritious fresh greens at farmstands! Try spinach, kale, Swiss chard, bok choy, broccoli rabe or peppery mustard greens. Add them to stir-fries or just simmer in broth with a little sautéed onion.

Baked Ziti with Spinach & Cheese *Makes 8 servings*

2 10-oz. pkgs. frozen chopped
  spinach
3 eggs, beaten
15-oz. container ricotta cheese
2/3 c. grated Parmesan cheese
1/4 t. pepper

16-oz. pkg. ziti pasta, cooked
28-oz. jar spaghetti sauce
2 t. dried oregano
12-oz. pkg. shredded mozzarella
  cheese

Cook spinach as package directs; drain, cool and squeeze out well. Place
spinach in a bowl. Add eggs, ricotta cheese, Parmesan cheese and
pepper; mix well and set aside. In a separate bowl, combine cooked
ziti with sauce and oregano. Place half the ziti mixture in a lightly
greased 13"x9" baking pan; layer with mozzarella cheese and spinach
mixture. Add remaining ziti mixture; cover with aluminum foil. Bake at
375 degrees for 25 minutes, or until bubbly. Let stand about 10 minutes
before serving.

For a no-fuss meatless meal, spoon grilled or roasted veggies onto a softened tortilla and roll up...delicious!

Black Bean & Pepper Enchiladas

Serves 4 to 6

1 T. oil
1 T. garlic, minced
2 green or red peppers, sliced
1 onion, sliced
15-oz. can black beans, drained
　　and rinsed

16-oz. can enchilada sauce,
　　divided
10 6-inch flour or corn tortillas
16-oz. pkg. shredded sharp
　　Cheddar cheese

Add oil to a skillet over medium heat. Sauté garlic, peppers and onion until onion is transparent. Remove from heat and place in a bowl; add beans. Pour half the enchilada sauce into a greased 13"x9" baking pan. Fill tortillas with 2 to 3 tablespoonfuls of vegetable mixture; sprinkle with cheese. Roll up tortillas and place seam-side down into baking pan. Top with remaining enchilada sauce and any remaining cheese. Bake, uncovered, at 350 degrees for 30 minutes, until heated through and cheese is melted.

A well-loved china teapot that's been handed down to you
makes a sweet vase for daisies, coreopsis, bachelor buttons,
zinnia and larkspur from the farmers' market.

Rigatoni with Cannellini & Kale

Serves 6

2-1/2 c. rigatoni pasta, uncooked
2 T. olive oil, divided
3 cloves garlic, minced
7-oz. jar roasted red peppers,
    drained and sliced
1/2 lb. kale, coarsely chopped and
    stems removed

16-oz. can cannellini beans,
    drained and rinsed
2 T. lemon juice
1/4 t. pepper
6 T. grated Parmesan cheese

Cook pasta according to package directions. Drain, reserving 1/4 cup cooking liquid; set aside. Meanwhile, heat one tablespoon oil in a Dutch oven over medium heat. Add garlic and peppers; sauté for one minute. Add kale and beans; cover and cook for 5 minutes, or until kale is wilted, stirring occasionally. Add cooked pasta, reserved cooking liquid, remaining oil, lemon juice and pepper; toss well. Sprinkle with Parmesan cheese.

Make a quick crumb crust for a savory quiche. Spread
2-1/2 tablespoons softened butter in a pie plate, then firmly
press 2-1/2 cups seasoned dry bread crumbs into the butter.
Freeze until firm, pour in filling and bake as directed.

Bountiful Garden Pie

Makes 6 to 8 servings

4 c. yellow squash, sliced
8-oz. pkg. sliced mushrooms
1 green pepper, sliced
1 red pepper, sliced
1 onion, sliced
1 clove garlic, minced
1/4 c. olive oil
1 t. salt

1/2 t. white pepper
1/8 t. cayenne pepper
4 eggs
1/2 c. half-and-half
1 c. Gruyère cheese, shredded
3/4 c. grated Parmesan cheese
9-inch pie crust

In a large skillet over medium-high heat, sauté vegetables for 10 minutes. Transfer vegetables with a slotted spoon to a bowl. Sprinkle with salt and peppers; stir until well blended. Beat together eggs and half-and-half; stir in cheeses. Pour 2/3 cup of egg mixture into crust. Spoon in half of the vegetables. Continue layering, ending with egg mixture. Bake at 375 degrees for 35 to 40 minutes, until top is golden and filling is set. Cool on rack for 30 minutes; cut into wedges and serve warm.

Take your family with you to the farmers' market.
Kids will love seeing all there is to enjoy...and a taste
of a warm ripe tomato or juicy peach is a real treat.

Grilled Vegetable Kabobs

1/2 c. Italian salad dressing
1 T. fresh parsley, minced
1 t. fresh basil, chopped
1/2 t. fresh chives, chopped
2 yellow squash, cut into
    one-inch thick slices

8 onions, sliced into wedges
8 cherry tomatoes
8 mushrooms
8 wooden skewers
2 c. cooked rice

Combine salad dressing and herbs in a small bowl; cover and chill. Alternate squash slices, onion wedges, tomatoes and mushrooms evenly among skewers. Brush with dressing mixture, reserving any excess, and set aside. Spray a grill rack with non-stick vegetable spray. Place skewers on grill over medium heat. Grill for 15 minutes, or until vegetables are tender, turning and basting frequently with reserved dressing mixture. To serve, place 1/2 cup cooked rice on each plate and top with 2 kabobs.

For healthy, filling meatless meals, try whole grains like
barley and brown rice. They're high in protein and, with the
addition of different seasonings, adapt readily to
many tasty flavors.

Laurie's Stuffed Peppers

Serves 4

4 green, red or yellow peppers
2 T. olive oil
8-oz. pkg. mushrooms, finely
    chopped
1 onion, finely chopped
1 clove garlic, pressed
1 c. cooked white rice

1 c. cooked brown rice
3 to 4 drops hot pepper sauce
salt and pepper
2 15-oz. cans tomato sauce,
    divided
1 c. shredded mozzarella cheese

Slice off tops of peppers; remove seeds. Fill a large soup pot with water; bring to a boil over medium-high heat. Add peppers; boil for 5 minutes. Remove peppers; set aside. Heat oil in a large skillet over medium heat; add mushrooms, onion and garlic. Sauté for 5 minutes, or until onion is tender. Add cooked rice, hot sauce, salt and pepper; cook for 2 minutes. Add one can tomato sauce and simmer for 5 minutes; spoon mixture into peppers. Spread 1/2 can tomato sauce in a greased 13"x9" baking pan. Place peppers in pan; spoon remaining sauce over top. Bake, uncovered, at 350 degrees for 25 minutes; sprinkle with cheese. Bake for an additional 10 minutes, or until cheese is melted.

A portable herb garden! Tuck several herb plants inside a vintage tin picnic basket...so easy to carry to the kitchen when it's time to snip fresh herbs.

Walnut-Parsley Pesto Linguine   *Makes 4 to 6 servings*

16-oz. pkg. linguine pasta,
   uncooked
2 c. fresh flat-leaf parsley,
   coarsely chopped
1 c. chopped walnuts, toasted
3/4 c. shredded Parmigiano-
   Reggiano cheese

1 c. green onions, thinly sliced
1 t. salt
1/2 c. olive oil
2 to 3 t. lemon juice
3 to 4 T. water
pepper to taste
Garnish: grated Parmesan cheese

Cook pasta according to package directions; drain. Meanwhile, place
parsley, walnuts, cheese, onions and salt in a food processor. Process
ingredients while slowly pouring in olive oil, until mixture forms a thick
paste. Continue to process while slowly adding lemon juice and water to
thin mixture to a smooth consistency. Toss with warm pasta and garnish
with Parmesan cheese; serve immediately.

Whenever you prepare winter squash for dinner, save the
seeds...they're delicious toasted. Rinse seeds and pat dry. Toss
with olive oil and coarse salt. Spread on an ungreased baking
sheet and bake for 12 to 15 minutes at 350 degrees.

Cheesy Baked Eggplant

Serves 6 to 8

1-lb. eggplant, peeled and cubed
1 c. dry bread crumbs
1/2 c. evaporated milk
1/4 c. milk
1/4 c. onion, minced
1/4 c. green pepper, minced
1/4 c. celery, minced

1/4 c. butter
2 eggs, beaten
1 T. chopped pimento, drained
2 t. salt
1/2 t. pepper
1/4 t. dried sage
1-1/2 c. shredded Cheddar cheese

Cover eggplant with water; refrigerate for at least 6 hours. Drain; place in a saucepan. Cover with fresh water; simmer over medium heat until tender and set aside. Soak bread crumbs in milks. In a skillet, sauté onion, pepper and celery in butter for 10 to 15 minutes. Stir in bread crumb mixture and drained eggplant. Add eggs, pimento, salt, pepper and sage; blend well. Spread in a greased 13"x9" baking pan. Bake, uncovered, at 350 degrees for 45 minutes. Sprinkle with cheese; bake an additional 5 to 6 minutes until cheese melts.

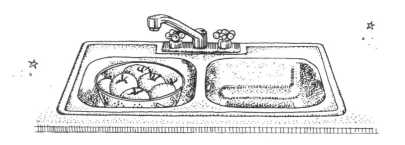

Use a damp brush sprinkled with baking soda
to scrub fruits & veggies...no fancy
produce wash needed!

Joan's Ratatoûille

2 c. onion, chopped
4 cloves garlic, minced
1/2 c. olive oil
8 c. tomatoes, peeled and coarsely
    chopped
4 to 6 c. zucchini, cut into
    1/2-inch thick slices

2 green peppers, cut into thin
    strips
2 red peppers, cut into thin strips
1 T. chili powder, or to taste
salt to taste

In a large saucepan or deep skillet over medium heat, sauté onion and
garlic in oil, about 3 to 4 minutes. Add tomatoes, zucchini and peppers.
Reduce heat; cover and simmer, stirring occasionally, until vegetables are
tender, about 20 minutes. Stir in seasonings. Simmer, uncovered, an
additional 15 minutes, stirring occasionally.

Serve up frosty lemonade or herbal ice tea
with blueberry skewers. Simply slide blueberries onto
a wooden skewer until covered; top with
a fresh mint leaf...easy!

Fast-Fix Pasta Primavera

3 c. frozen mixed vegetables,
    thawed
2 T. olive oil
16-oz. pkg. fettuccine pasta,
    uncooked

1/2 c. butter, sliced
1/2 to 1 c. grated Parmesan
    cheese
1 c. whipping cream
salt and pepper to taste

In a skillet over medium heat, sauté vegetables in oil until crisp-tender. Meanwhile, cook pasta according to package directions; drain and return to pot. Add butter to melt. Stir in sautéed vegetables and remaining ingredients to pasta; toss to mix well.

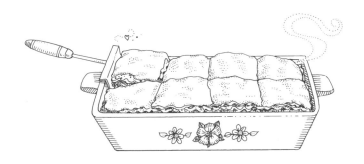

For a delicious, healthy change from regular pasta,
make "noodles" from zucchini or summer squash. Cut the
squash into long, thin strips, steam lightly or sauté in
a little olive oil and toss with your favorite pasta sauce.

White Lasagna

8-oz. pkg. lasagna noodles,
    uncooked
3 T. butter
1 t. lemon juice
16-oz. pkg. sliced mushrooms
1/4 c. all-purpose flour

1 t. salt
1/8 t. cayenne pepper
2-1/2 c. milk
2 T. fresh parsley, chopped
16-oz. container ricotta cheese
1/2 c. grated Parmesan cheese

Cook noodles according to package directions; drain. Meanwhile, melt
butter in a large skillet over medium heat. Stir in lemon juice and sauté
mushrooms until tender. Stir in flour, salt and cayenne pepper. Gradually
stir in milk. Cook until slightly thickened; stir in parsley. Spread half
the mushroom mixture in a lightly greased 13"x9" baking pan.
Alternate layers of noodles and ricotta cheese, ending with ricotta.
Top with remaining mushroom mixture. Sprinkle with Parmesan cheese.
Bake, covered, at 350 degrees for 45 minutes. Let stand 15 minutes
before serving.

Make 'em mini! Prepare Crustless Zucchini Pie in mini muffin
cups for individual servings... just decrease baking time
by 10 minutes. Top each with a dainty dollop of
sour cream and a sprig of dill. So pretty!

Crustless Zucchini Pie

Makes 16 servings

1 onion, finely chopped
1/2 c. oil
1/2 c. grated Parmesan cheese
4 eggs, beaten

1 T. fresh parsley, minced
3 c. zucchini, shredded
1 c. biscuit baking mix
1 c. shredded Cheddar cheese

In a large bowl, combine onion, oil, Parmesan cheese, eggs and parsley. Mix well; stir in remaining ingredients. Pour into two 9" pie plates that have been sprayed with non-stick vegetable spray. Bake at 350 degrees for 35 to 45 minutes, until golden. Let stand for 10 minutes; slice into wedges and serve warm.

He who enjoys good health is rich,
though he knows it not.

—Italian Proverb

Lentil & Brown Rice Tacos

Serves 6 to 8

1 T. olive oil
1/2 c. onion, diced
1 to 2 cloves garlic, minced
2 t. chili powder
1/2 t. ground cumin
3/4 c. long-cooking brown rice, uncooked
3/4 c. dried brown lentils, uncooked

4 c. vegetable broth
salt and pepper to taste
6 to 8 6-inch corn or flour tortillas
Garnish: shredded lettuce, sliced avocado, diced tomatoes, sour cream, salsa, shredded Cheddar cheese

Heat olive oil in a saucepan over medium heat. Sauté onion for about 4 minutes. Add garlic and spices; cook for about one minute to toast spices. Add rice; stir to coat rice in spices. Add lentils and broth; bring to a boil. Reduce heat to a simmer; cover and cook for about 45 to 50 minutes, until rice and lentils are tender. Remove from heat; fluff with a fork and season with salt and pepper. Spoon mixture into tortillas and top with your favorite taco fixings.

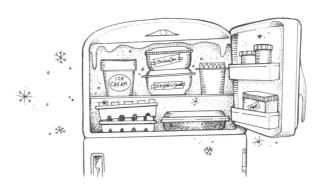

Enjoy a taste of summer in fall...make an extra of
a favorite veggie casserole to tuck in the freezer.
Wrap well with plastic wrap and freeze. Thaw overnight
in the refrigerator and bake as usual.

Farmstand Veggie Roast

Makes 6 to 8 servings

1 lb. baby carrots
1 onion, cut into wedges
1/3 c. olive oil
2 t. Italian seasoning
1 t. garlic, minced
1 t. salt
1/4 t. pepper
1/2 t. sugar

2-1/2 c. cauliflower, cut into
  flowerets
1 zucchini, sliced 1/4-inch thick
1 yellow squash, sliced 1/4-inch
  thick
1-1/2 c. asparagus, cut into
  1-inch pieces

Place carrots and onion in a large slow cooker; set aside. In a small bowl, mix olive oil and seasonings. Pour half of oil mixture into slow cooker; toss to coat. Cover and cook on high setting for 2 to 2-1/2 hours, until tender. Toss together remaining oil mixture and remaining vegetables; add to slow cooker. Cover and cook on high setting an additional 30 to 45 minutes, until crisp-tender.

The crisper bin of the fridge is designed to keep
fruits & veggies fresh and tasty. There are just a few
exceptions...store potatoes, sweet potatoes, onions and
winter squash in a bin at room temperature.

Bean Pot Medley

15-oz. can black beans
15-oz. can kidney beans
15-oz. can Great Northern beans
15-oz. can garbanzo beans

15-oz. can black-eyed peas
1 c. green pepper, chopped
1 c. red pepper, chopped
1 c. onion, chopped

Drain and rinse all the beans and peas in a colander. Pour into a large plastic bowl with a lid; add peppers and onion. Cover bowl and shake until blended. Pour half of Sauce over beans, cover and shake; add remaining sauce and shake again. Pour into a slow cooker; cover and cook on low setting for 5 to 6 hours. Stir again before serving.

Sauce:

1-1/2 c. catsup
1/2 c. brown sugar, packed
2 T. dried basil

1 t. dry mustard
1/8 t. pepper
2 to 3 t. red wine vinegar

Mix together all ingredients in a bowl.

Save time when peeling and chopping veggies.
Set a large bowl on the counter to toss all
the peelings into...you'll only need to carry it
once to the compost bin or wastebasket.

Louisiana Red Beans & Rice

Makes 6 servings

2 15-oz. cans red beans
14-1/2 oz. can diced tomatoes
1/2 c. celery, chopped
1/2 c. green pepper, chopped
1/2 c. green onions, chopped

2 cloves garlic, minced
1 to 2 t. hot pepper sauce
1 t. Worcestershire sauce
1 bay leaf
cooked rice

Combine all ingredients except rice in a slow cooker; do not drain beans and tomatoes. Cover and cook on low setting for 4 to 6 hours. About 30 minutes before serving, use a potato masher to mash mixture slightly until thickened. Cover again; increase heat to high setting and continue cooking for 30 minutes. Discard bay leaf. To serve, ladle over cooked rice in bowls.

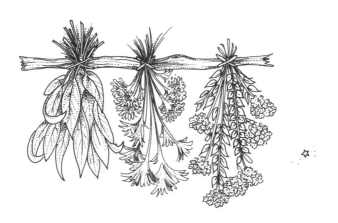

Fresh veggies are delicious simply steamed and
topped with pats of chive butter. To make, blend 1/4 cup
softened butter with 2 tablespoons chopped fresh chives,
one teaspoon lemon zest and a little salt & pepper.
Try other favorite herbs too.

Broiled Parmesan Tomatoes

Makes 6 servings

3 tomatoes, halved
1 T. olive oil
1 clove garlic, minced
1/4 t. pepper

1 T. fresh basil, minced
3/4 c. soft bread crumbs
2 T. grated Parmesan cheese

Arrange tomato halves cut-side up on a broiler pan sprayed with non-stick vegetable spray; set aside. Combine oil, garlic and pepper; brush over tomatoes and sprinkle with basil. Broil about 6 inches from heat for 3 to 4 minutes, until heated through. In a small bowl, combine bread crumbs and Parmesan cheese; sprinkle over tomatoes. Broil an additional one to 2 minutes, until crumbs are golden. Serve immediately.

If you have a small family, or if there's just the two of you at home, pick up a vintage divided serving dish or two...they're just right for serving up lots of sides without crowding the table.

Mashed Root Vegetables

1/2 lb. sweet potatoes, peeled and cubed
1/2 lb. parsnips, peeled and cubed
1/2 lb. celery root, peeled and cubed

2 to 3 T. olive oil
salt and pepper to taste
1 lb. potatoes, peeled and cubed
3 T. butter, softened
1/2 c. milk

In a bowl, toss together sweet potatoes, parsnips and celery root with oil, salt and pepper. Place on an ungreased 15"x10" jelly-roll pan. Bake at 350 degrees for 20 to 25 minutes, until golden. Meanwhile, place potatoes in a large saucepan and cover with salted water. Bring to a boil over medium-high heat; reduce heat to medium and cook until tender, about 12 to 15 minutes. Drain; return potatoes to the pot. Add roasted vegetables and butter; mash and stir until butter melts. Add milk; stir to mix. Season to taste with additional salt and pepper, if desired.

Cooked, mashed sweet potatoes, pumpkin and butternut squash can be used interchangeably in quick breads, pies, soups and other everyday dishes. Try out a different combination and discover a whole new taste!

Sweet Potato Toss

2 sweet potatoes, peeled and
    sliced
4 potatoes, peeled and sliced
1/2 to 1 T. onion powder

1/8 t. sugar
salt to taste
canola oil for frying

Combine all potato slices in a bowl; toss with seasonings. Into a skillet over medium-high heat, add oil to 1/2-inch depth. Add potatoes to hot oil in skillet. Cover and cook, turning as needed. Reduce heat to medium when potatoes begin to soften. Uncover for the last 3 to 4 minutes of cooking to crisp up potatoes.

Don't hesitate to stock up on frozen vegetables.
Flash-frozen soon after being harvested, they retain
more nutrients than fresh produce that has traveled
for several days before arriving in the
grocery's produce aisle.

Scotch Limas

Makes 6 to 8 servings

16-oz. pkg. dried lima beans
4 c. water
1 onion, chopped
1/4 c. celery, diced

6 T. butter, melted
1/3 c. brown sugar, packed
1/2 clove garlic, finely chopped
2 t. salt

Cover beans with water and soak overnight. In the morning, drain beans and place in a large saucepan. Add 4 cups water and remaining ingredients. Bring to a boil over medium-high heat. Reduce heat; cover and simmer for one hour to 1-1/4 hours, stirring occasionally, until beans are tender. Transfer mixture to a well-greased 2-quart casserole dish. Bake, uncovered, at 350 degrees for 20 minutes, or until heated through.

For the tastiest results, reduce the oven temperature
by 25 degrees if you're using glass or dark metal
baking pans...they retain heat more than
shiny metal pans do.

Roasted Garden Flatbreads

Serves 2 to 4

2 naan flatbreads or pita rounds
3 T. olive oil, divided
1 zucchini, quartered and sliced
1 c. baby portabella mushrooms,
   sliced
1/2 c. marinated artichoke hearts,
   drained
1/4 c. sliced black olives, drained

1/4 red onion, chopped
1 t. salt
1/4 t. pepper
2 T. Italian seasoning, divided
1/2 c. cream cheese, softened
1/4 c. grated Parmesan cheese
8 slices tomato
4 slices provolone cheese

Brush flatbreads or pitas with one tablespoon oil; place on an ungreased baking sheet. Bake at 400 degrees for 5 minutes, or until lightly golden. Cool on a wire rack. Increase oven to 425 degrees. Add all vegetables except tomato to baking sheet. Sprinkle with salt, pepper and one tablespoon Italian seasoning. Drizzle lightly with remaining oil and toss to coat. Bake until vegetables start to soften, about 20 minutes. In a bowl, blend cheeses and remaining Italian seasoning; spread over cooled flatbreads. Divide roasted vegetables between flatbreads; spread to cover. Arrange tomato and cheese slices on top. Bake an additional 6 to 7 minutes, until crisp and golden.

Make tangy pickled veggies next time you finish a jar
of pickles! Simply cut up raw carrots, green peppers,
celery and other vegetables, drop them into
the leftover pickle juice and refrigerate.

Mom's Eggplant Sandwich

Serves 4

1 eggplant, sliced 1/2-inch thick
2 zucchini or yellow squash,
    sliced 1/2-inch thick
salt and pepper to taste
2 T. olive oil
3 to 4 T. mayonnaise

1 French baguette loaf, halved
    lengthwise
1 tomato, thinly sliced
1/4 c. grated Parmesan cheese,
    divided

Sprinkle eggplant and squash slices with salt and pepper; set aside. Heat oil in a grill pan over medium heat. Grill eggplant and squash until veggies are tender and have grill marks; drain on a paper towel. Spread mayonnaise over cut sides of loaf. Arrange tomato slices on bottom half; sprinkle with salt, pepper and half of Parmesan cheese. Layer grilled eggplant and squash on top of tomatoes. Sprinkle with remaining cheese and add top half; slice into quarters.

Watch for whimsical diner-style sectioned plates
at tag sales. They're perfect for serving up
Southern-style vegetable plates...the sections
keep veggie dishes and cornbread separate.

Toasted Green Tomato Sandwiches

Serves 4

1-1/2 to 2 c. cornmeal
seasoning salt and pepper to taste
2 green tomatoes, sliced 1/4-inch
   thick

1/4 c. oil
2 to 3 T. butter, softened
8 slices whole-wheat bread

Combine cornmeal and seasonings in a large plastic zipping bag. Shake to mix well. Add tomato slices and gently shake to coat. Remove from bag, shaking off excess cornmeal mixture. Heat oil in a large skillet over medium heat; fry tomatoes until golden on both sides. Remove from skillet. Spread butter on one side of each slice. Arrange 4 slices, butter-side down, in skillet. Top with tomato slices and remaining bread, butter-side up. Cook over medium heat, turning once, until golden on both sides.

Stir up some lemonade for dinner...it couldn't be simpler!
In a saucepan, combine 2 quarts water and 1/2 cup sugar.
Cook and stir just until sugar dissolves. Remove from heat
and add 3/4 cup fresh lemon juice. Mix well and chill.

Roasted Veggie Panini

2 zucchini, thickly sliced
1 yellow squash, thickly sliced
8-oz. pkg. portabella mushrooms
2 t. olive oil, divided
1 t. balsamic vinegar
1 sweet onion, sliced
8 slices sourdough bread

1/4 c. olive tapenade
1 red pepper, thickly sliced
1 green pepper, thickly sliced
1 yellow pepper, thickly sliced
1 c. spinach leaves
2 roma tomatoes, sliced
4 slices provolone cheese

Combine zucchini, squash and mushrooms in a large bowl; toss with one teaspoon olive oil and vinegar. Grill or broil until tender and golden; set aside. In a skillet over medium heat, cook onion in remaining olive oil until caramelized, about 15 minutes; set aside. Spread tops and bottoms of bread slices with olive tapenade; layer fillings evenly on half the bread slices. Top with remaining bread slices; grill or broil lightly on both sides.

Sweet potato chips...yummy! Peel sweet potatoes, slice thinly
and toss with oil. Bake on a baking sheet at 400 degrees
for 22 to 25 minutes, turning once. Sprinkle with
cinnamon-sugar and serve warm.

Irene's Portabella Burgers

Serves 4

4 portabella mushroom caps
1 c. Italian salad dressing
4 sourdough buns, split

4 slices Muenster or Gruyère
  cheese
Garnish: romaine lettuce

Combine mushrooms and salad dressing in a plastic zipping bag, turning to coat. Chill 30 minutes, turning occasionally. Remove mushrooms, discarding dressing. Grill mushrooms, covered with grill lid, over medium heat for 2 to 3 minutes on each side. Grill buns, cut-side down, one minute, or until toasted. Top buns with mushroom, cheese and lettuce; serve immediately.

A big chalkboard in the kitchen is a
handy spot to keep a running grocery list.

Annelle's Special Veggie Melts

Makes 4 servings

1 c. sliced baby portabella
    mushrooms
1/4 c. olive oil
1 loaf focaccia bread, halved
    horizontally

15-oz. jar whole roasted red
    peppers, drained
1-1/2 t. Italian seasoning
1 c. shredded Fontina cheese

In a skillet over medium heat, sauté mushrooms in olive oil until tender. Place bread halves, cut-side up, on an ungreased baking sheet. On one bread half, layer peppers, mushrooms and Italian seasoning. Top both halves evenly with cheese. Broil until lightly golden. Assemble sandwich and cut into 4 pieces.

Bread bowls make a hearty soup special. Cut the tops off round bread loaves and hollow out, then rub with olive oil and garlic. Slip into the oven for 10 minutes at 400 degrees, until crusty and golden. Ladle in soup and serve right away.

Vegetarian Cincinnati Chili

Serves 6

46-oz. can tomato juice
16-oz. can kidney beans, drained
    and rinsed
1 onion, chopped
2 T. chili powder
1-1/2 t. white vinegar
1 t. allspice
1 t. cinnamon

1 t. pepper
1 t. ground cumin
1/8 t. garlic powder
1/4 t. Worcestershire sauce
5 bay leaves
cooked spaghetti
Garnish: shredded Cheddar
    cheese

Combine all ingredients except spaghetti and garnish in a slow cooker. Cover and cook on low setting for 5 hours. Discard bay leaves. Serve chili over cooked spaghetti, topped with cheese.

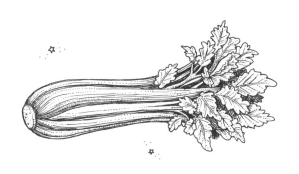

Don't toss out the leaves from fresh celery...
they're full of flavor! Lay them on a paper towel
where they'll dry in just a day or two.
Store the dried leaves in a canning jar
to toss into soups and stews.

Homestyle Vegetable Soup & Dumplings   *Serves 4*

1/2 c. onion, chopped
1 T. oil
1/2 c. rosamarina or orzo pasta, uncooked
4 c. vegetable broth
1 t. dry mustard
16-oz. pkg. frozen peas, potatoes and carrots, thawed

15-1/2 oz. can Great Northern beans, drained and rinsed
1 c. biscuit baking mix
2/3 c. cornmeal
1/4 t. dried oregano
1/4 t. dried basil
2/3 c. milk

In a large saucepan over medium heat, sauté onion in oil until tender, about 5 minutes. Stir in pasta, broth, mustard, vegetables and beans; heat to boiling, stirring occasionally. In a bowl, stir together baking mix, cornmeal and herbs; stir in milk just until moistened. Drop dough by tablespoonfuls onto boiling stew; reduce heat to low. Cook, uncovered, for 10 minutes. Cover and cook an additional 10 minutes.

Make your own yogurt cheese...it's simple!
Spoon plain unsweetened yogurt into a cheesecloth-lined
colander and set it in a bowl. Cover with plastic wrap and
refrigerate overnight. The next day, season the
fresh cheese with salt, pepper and dill or chives. Mmm!

Creamy Root Vegetable Soup

Serves 4 to 6

2 T. butter, diced
3 to 4 Yukon Gold potatoes,
   peeled and cubed
3 to 4 carrots, peeled and sliced
2 turnips, peeled and cubed
2 parsnips, peeled and sliced
1 rutabaga, peeled and cubed

1 to 2 leeks, sliced
2 to 3 cloves garlic, minced
14-1/2 oz. can chicken broth
8-oz. container sour cream
salt and pepper to taste
Garnish: sour cream, chopped
   fresh chives

Spray a 13"x9" glass baking pan with non-stick vegetable spray. Scatter butter in pan; arrange vegetables over top and sprinkle with garlic. Bake, uncovered, at 400 degrees for one hour, turning once, or until vegetables are tender. Set aside. In a large saucepan, bring broth to a boil over medium heat. Spoon in 3/4 of the vegetables and purée with an immersion blender. Add remaining vegetables; heat through. Stir in sour cream; add salt and pepper to taste. Garnish servings with a dollop of sour cream and a sprinkle of chives.

Use seed packet clippings to embellish a small notebook...
oh-so handy for making shopping lists or keeping
schedules. Tie up a stack with ribbon for gift giving.

Slow-Cooker Sweet Potato Chili

Serves 6

28-oz. can diced tomatoes
16-oz. can black beans, drained
    and rinsed
16-oz. can kidney beans, drained
    and rinsed
1 onion, chopped
1 red pepper, chopped
1 green pepper, chopped

3 to 4 stalks celery, chopped
2 sweet potatoes, peeled and cut
    into 1/2-inch cubes
Optional: canned diced jalapeños
    or hot pepper sauce to taste
8-oz. pkg. shredded Mexican-
    blend or Cheddar cheese

Combine all ingredients except cheese in a slow cooker; stir to mix. Cover and cook on low setting for 8 to 10 hours, or on high setting for 4 to 5 hours. Garnish with cheese.

Blanching makes fresh veggies crisp and bright...super for salads and dips. Bring a large pot of salted water to a rolling boil, add trimmed veggies and boil for 3 to 4 minutes, just until they begin to soften. Immediately remove veggies to a bowl of ice water. Cool, drain and pat dry.

Fresh Minestrone Soup

Makes 6 servings

3 leeks, chopped
3 cloves garlic, minced
2 T. olive oil
8 c. vegetable broth
15-1/2 oz. can kidney beans
2 c. potatoes, peeled and chopped
1 c. carrots, peeled and chopped
1/2 c. celery, chopped
1-1/2 c. yellow squash, chopped

2 c. green beans, sliced
1/2 t. dried basil
1/2 t. dried oregano
1/2 t. dried rosemary
salt and pepper to taste
1/4 c. tomato paste
1/2 c. ditalini pasta, uncooked
Garnish: shredded Parmesan
cheese

In a stockpot over medium heat, sauté leeks and garlic in oil for 3 to 5 minutes; drain. Add broth, beans with liquid, vegetables and seasonings; bring to a boil. Reduce heat to low; simmer for 30 minutes. Stir in tomato paste and uncooked pasta. Cook for an additional 15 minutes, or until pasta is tender. Serve topped with Parmesan cheese.

Make a warm loaf of crostini...so tasty with soup. Slice a loaf of
Italian bread into 1/2-inch slices. Brush olive oil over both sides
of each slice; sprinkle with coarse salt. Bake in a 300-degree
oven for 20 minutes, or until toasty, turning once.

Vegetable Ribolitta

Serves 8

1 c. sweet onion, chopped
2/3 c. celery, chopped
2/3 c. baby carrots, sliced
3 to 4 cloves garlic, minced
2 T. olive oil
2 19-oz. cans cannellini beans,
    drained and rinsed
32-oz. can vegetable broth
4 c. cabbage, chopped

2 14-1/2 oz. cans diced Italian
    tomatoes
1/2 c. zucchini, diced
1/4 c. red pepper, diced
1/4 c. yellow pepper, diced
1 t. fresh thyme, chopped
Garnish: crostini slices,
    grated Parmesan cheese

In a stockpot over medium heat, sauté onion, celery, carrots and garlic in olive oil until tender, about 5 minutes. Add remaining ingredients except garnish. Simmer for about 20 minutes, or until vegetables are tender. To serve, place a slice of crostini in each bowl and ladle soup into bowl. Sprinkle with Parmesan cheese.

Need to add a little zing to a soup or stew? Just add
a dash of herb-flavored vinegar...a super use for that
bottle you brought home from the farmers' market!

Spicy Vegetable Soup

Makes 8 servings

2 T. olive oil
2 onions, sliced
2 cloves garlic, minced
6 c. vegetable broth
1 c. celery, chopped
1 c. cauliflower flowerets
1 c. broccoli flowerets
1-1/2 c. green beans, sliced

4-oz. can diced green chiles
2 T. chili powder
1 T. dried oregano
1 T. ground cumin
1 t. paprika
1 t. ground sage
Garnish: herbed croutons

Heat oil in a large skillet over medium-high heat. Add onions and garlic; sauté until onions are tender, about 5 minutes. Transfer to a slow cooker. Add remaining ingredients except croutons, stirring to combine. Cover and cook on low setting for 6 to 7 hours. Serve soup topped with croutons.

Slow-cook a pot of creamy beans. Rinse and drain 1/2 pound dried navy beans. Place them in a slow cooker and stir in a chopped onion, a tablespoon of olive oil and 5 cups boiling water. Cover and cook on high setting for 4 hours, stirring occasionally. Don't add any tomatoes or salt until the beans are tender. So easy!

Vegetarian 3-Bean Chili

Makes 8 servings

1 onion, chopped
1 green pepper, chopped
4 cloves garlic, minced
2 t. olive oil
14-1/2 oz. can vegetable broth
16-oz. can kidney beans, drained
   and rinsed
16-oz. can black beans, drained
   and rinsed

16-oz. can fat-free refried beans
14-1/2 oz. can stewed tomatoes,
   chopped
3/4 c. salsa
2 t. chili powder
1/2 t. pepper
1/4 t. ground cumin
Garnish: saltine crackers

In a large saucepan over medium heat, sauté onion, green pepper and
garlic in oil until tender. Add remaining ingredients except crackers;
mix well. Bring to a boil. Reduce heat; cover and simmer for 10 to
15 minutes. Serve with crackers.

Give any chunky veggie or bean soup a creamier texture...
no cream required! Use a hand-held immersion blender to
purée some of the cooked veggies right in the saucepan.

7-Veggie Slow-Cooker Stew

Serves 10

1 butternut squash, peeled,
    seeded and cubed
2 c. eggplant, peeled and cubed
2 c. zucchini, diced
10-oz. pkg. frozen okra, thawed
8-oz. can tomato sauce
1 c. onion, chopped
1 tomato, chopped

1 carrot, peeled and thinly sliced
1/2 c. vegetable broth
1 clove garlic, chopped
1/2 t. ground cumin
1/2 t. turmeric
1/4 t. red pepper flakes
1/4 t. cinnamon
1/4 t. paprika

Combine all ingredients in a slow cooker. Cover and cook on low setting
for 8 to 10 hours, or until vegetables are tender.

Don't toss out the stalks when preparing fresh broccoli...they're good to eat too. Peel stalks with a potato peeler, then chop or dice and add to salads, stir-fries and baked dishes.

Colby-Swiss Broccoli Soup

Serves 6

1/2 c. water
1-1/2 t. chicken bouillon granules
4 c. broccoli flowerets
1 c. carrots, peeled and sliced
3 T. butter
1/4 c. green onions, sliced

3 T. all-purpose flour
1/4 to 1/2 t. nutmeg
1/4 t. pepper
3 c. milk
2 c. shredded Colby cheese
1 c. shredded Swiss cheese

Combine water and bouillon in a 3-quart saucepan; bring to a boil over medium heat. Add broccoli and carrots; return to a boil. Reduce heat; cover and cook for about 10 minutes, until vegetables are tender. Drain, reserving liquid. Set aside. Melt butter; add onion and cook until tender. Stir in flour, nutmeg and pepper. Cook for one minute; gradually add milk and reserved liquid. Cook until thickened; stir in broccoli mixture. Sprinkle in cheeses. Stir until cheeses are melted

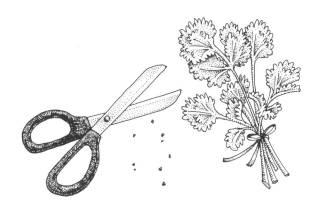

Kitchen shears are oh-so handy for snipping fresh herbs,
chopping green onions and snipping the ends off fresh
green beans. Just remember to wash them with
soap and water after each use.

Spinach, Strawberry & Walnut Salad

Makes 6 servings

1-1/2 lbs. spinach, torn
3 c. strawberries, hulled and
    sliced

1 sweet onion, thinly sliced
1 c. chopped walnuts

Arrange spinach, strawberries, onions and nuts in a salad bowl. Cover and refrigerate. At serving time, drizzle desired amount of Poppy Seed Dressing over salad. Toss and serve immediately.

Poppy Seed Dressing:

3/4 c. sugar
1 t. dry mustard
1 t. salt
1/3 c. cider vinegar

2 t. green onion, chopped
3/4 to 1 c. olive oil
1-1/2 T. poppy seed

In a blender, mix sugar, mustard, salt and vinegar until smooth. Add onion and blend until smooth. With blender running, add oil slowly. Blend until thick. Stir in poppy seed.

It's easy to tote a salad to a picnic. Mix it up in a plastic
zipping bag, seal and set it right in the cooler. When you
arrive at the picnic grounds, simply tip the salad
into a serving bowl.

Crunchy Pecan Salad

Serves 6 to 8

12-oz. pkg. shredded broccoli
    slaw mix
1-1/2 c. seedless red grapes,
    halved

1-1/2 c. Gala apples, peeled, cored
    and chopped
1/2 c. citrus salad dressing
3/4 c. chopped pecans

Combine broccoli, grapes and apples in a serving bowl. Drizzle with
dressing; toss gently to coat. Sprinkle with pecans before serving.

Write it on your heart that every day
is the best day of the year.

—Ralph Waldo Emerson

Veggie Delight Salad

Makes 10 servings

16-oz. pkg. shredded cabbage
1 c. carrots, peeled and grated
1/2 c. broccoli, chopped
1/2 c. cherry tomatoes, halved
1/2 c. celery, sliced

1/2 c. cucumber, peeled and diced
1/3 c. olive oil
2 T. vinegar
1 T. Dijon mustard
1 t. garlic salt

Combine vegetables in a large salad bowl. In a bowl, whisk together
remaining ingredients; drizzle over vegetables. Toss to coat. Serve chilled.

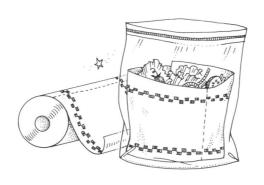

Keep salad greens crisp for up to a week. As soon as
you bring them home, rinse them in cool water,
wrap in paper towels and and slip into a plastic zipping
bag with several small holes cut in it. Tuck the bag in
the fridge's crisper bin...ready to enjoy anytime!

Artichoke-Tortellini Salad

Serves 6

7-oz. pkg. refrigerated cheese
    tortellini, uncooked
6-oz. jar marinated artichoke
    hearts
1 c. broccoli flowerets
1/2 c. fresh parsley, finely
    chopped
1 T. chopped pimento, drained

2 green onions, chopped
2-1/2 t. fresh basil, chopped
1/2 t. garlic powder
1/2 c. Italian salad dressing
5 to 6 cherry tomatoes, halved
Garnish: sliced black olives,
    grated Parmesan cheese

Cook tortellini according to package directions. Drain and rinse with cool water. In a large bowl, combine tortellini, artichokes with marinade and remaining ingredients except tomatoes and garnish. Cover and refrigerate 4 to 6 hours to blend flavors. When ready to serve, add tomatoes and toss lightly. Garnish with olives and cheese.

Mix up a zesty Dijon dressing in an almost-empty mustard jar...it's easy! Add 1/2 cup olive oil and 1/3 cup fresh lemon juice to the jar; shake well. Add salt and pepper to taste. Keep chilled.

Panzanella Bread Salad

Serves 4 to 6

4 c. day-old Italian bread, torn
    into bite-size pieces
5 tomatoes, diced
1/2 red onion, sliced
1/2 cucumber, peeled, quartered
    and sliced

1/2 c. fresh basil, chopped
3 cloves garlic, minced
3 T. red wine vinegar
1/4 c. olive oil
1/2 t. salt
pepper to taste

Combine bread, vegetables, basil and garlic; toss well. Sprinkle with
vinegar, oil, salt and pepper. Let stand at room temperature for 1-1/2 to
2 hours before serving, so the bread can absorb the dressing. Serve
immediately.

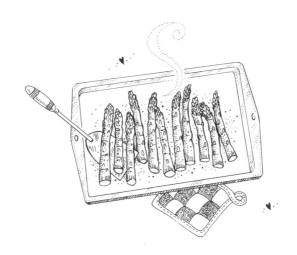

Roasted or grilled vegetables are delicious warm or cold.
Toss sliced veggies with olive oil and spread on a baking
sheet. Bake at 350 degrees, stirring occasionally,
for about 30 minutes, until tender.

Mediterranean Pasta Salad

12-oz. pkg. bow-tie pasta,
  uncooked
12-oz. jar marinated artichoke
  hearts, drained and chopped
2-1/4 oz. can sliced black olives,
  drained

1 cucumber, chopped
2 c. cherry tomatoes
3 T. sweet onion, chopped
8-oz. bottle balsamic vinaigrette
  salad dressing
6-oz. pkg. crumbled feta cheese

Cook pasta according to package directions. Drain and rinse with cool water. In a large bowl, toss together pasta and remaining ingredients except cheese. Cover and refrigerate for 2 to 3 hours. Before serving, toss with cheese.

For hearty salads in a snap, keep cans of diced tomatoes,
beans, black olives and marinated artichokes in the fridge.
They'll be chilled and ready to toss with fresh greens
at a moment's notice.

Corn, Black Bean & Avocado Salad

Serves 4 to 6

15-oz. can black beans, drained
   and rinsed
15-oz. can shoepeg corn, drained
1 avocado, halved, pitted and
   diced
6 green onions, thinly sliced
2 c. tomatoes, chopped, or cherry
   tomatoes, halved

Optional: 1/2 c. chopped fresh
   cilantro
1/2 c. lime vinaigrette salad
   dressing
salt and pepper to taste

In a large bowl, combine beans, corn, avocado, onions, tomatoes and cilantro, if using. Pour vinaigrette over salad. Add salt and pepper to taste. Stir salad to coat vegetables with dressing; cover and chill until serving.

Substitute roasted, salted pecans for crispy bacon
as a salad topping for a similar salty-smoky
taste and crunch.

Dill Vegetable Salad

3 cucumbers, peeled and thinly
  sliced
2 c. cherry tomatoes, halved
1/4 sweet onion, finely chopped
3/4 c. lemon juice

1/2 c. olive oil
3 T. honey
1 t. dill weed
1/2 t. garlic powder
1/8 t. salt

Place cucumbers, tomatoes and onion in a large bowl. In a separate bowl, whisk together remaining ingredients; drizzle over cucumber mixture. Toss to coat. Cover and refrigerate overnight.

Inexpensive light olive oil is just fine for cooking.
Save the extra-virgin olive oil for making salad dressings,
where its delicate flavor can be enjoyed.

Smoky Vegetable Pizzas

Makes 12 servings

1 red onion, thinly sliced into
  wedges
6-oz. jar marinated artichoke
  hearts, drained, quartered and
  marinade reserved
1 loaf frozen bread dough,
  thawed

2 c. smoked Gouda cheese,
  shredded and divided
3 roma tomatoes, sliced
4 green onions, thinly sliced
2 t. Italian seasoning
1 T. fresh basil, snipped

Place onion wedges on a lightly greased baking sheet. Brush with
reserved marinade. Bake at 425 degrees for 10 minutes; remove from
oven. Divide thawed dough into 12 balls. On a lightly floured surface,
flatten each ball to a 4-inch circle. Place dough circles on lightly greased
baking sheets; pierce with a fork. Sprinkle one cup cheese evenly over
dough circles. Top each with an onion wedge, an artichoke quarter and a
tomato slice. Sprinkle with sliced green onion, seasoning and remaining
cheese. Bake at 425 degrees for about 10 minutes, until edges are lightly
golden. Remove from oven; sprinkle with basil.

Bring along a tasty appetizer to the next gathering!
Tuck a loaf of pumpernickel bread filled with a yummy dip
into a basket, surround with bread cubes and snacking
crackers and deliver to your hostess...she'll love it!

Mama's Pizza Fondue

Makes about 4 cups

28-oz. jar meatless spaghetti
    sauce
8-oz. pkg. shredded mozzarella
    cheese
1/4 c. shredded Parmesan cheese

2 t. dried oregano
1 t. dried, minced onion
Optional: 1/4 t. garlic powder
1 loaf Italian bread, cubed

In a slow cooker, combine all ingredients except bread. Cover and cook
for 4 to 6 hours, until cheese is melted and sauce is hot. Serve warm in
slow cooker, with bread cubes for dipping.

Try using flavored wraps instead of tortillas for
roll-ups...sun-dried tomato-basil, garlic-herb or cilantro
really give them a zippy new taste.

Party-Perfect Pinwheels

Makes about 40 servings

2 8-oz. pkgs. cream cheese,
  softened
4 green onions, chopped
1-oz. pkg. ranch salad dressing
  mix
5 12-inch flour tortillas
3/4 c. green olives with pimentos,
  chopped

3/4 c. chopped black olives,
  drained
4-1/2 oz. can chopped green
  chiles, drained
4-oz. jar chopped pimentos,
  drained
Garnish: fresh parsley, chopped

In a bowl, blend cream cheese, onions and dressing mix. Spread evenly over one side of each tortilla. Stir together remaining ingredients; spoon over cream cheese mixture. Roll up each tortilla jelly-roll style; wrap each in plastic wrap. Refrigerate for at least 2 hours; cut into one-inch slices and garnish with parsley.

Try something new with your next bowl of dip!
Baby carrots, celery stalks, cherry tomatoes and
broccoli flowerets are all tasty dippers. Even lightly
steamed green beans, snow peas and asparagus spears
are crunchy and full of flavor.

Fast & Easy Red Pepper Hummus

Makes 2 cups

2 15-oz. cans chickpeas, drained
    and rinsed
2 T. taco seasoning mix

1 c. roasted red peppers, chopped
olive oil to taste

Purèe chickpeas, taco seasoning and roasted red peppers together in a food processor. Drizzle in olive oil until desired consistency is reached. Cover and chill one hour before serving. Serve with pita chips.

Homebaked Pita Chips:

6 pita rounds, halved and split   1 T. kosher salt

Cut each pita half into 8 to 12 wedges. Arrange on an aluminum foil-lined baking sheet. Spray chips with non-stick vegetable spray; sprinkle with salt. Broil for 3 to 5 minutes, until golden.

Throw an apron party! Invite your best girlfriends to
tie on their frilliest vintage aprons and join you
in the kitchen to whip up a favorite dish together.
It's a fun way to catch up with everyone.

Stuffed Pepper Wedges

1/2 c. chive & onion-flavored
   cream cheese spread
1 T. chopped black olives, drained

2 green, red or yellow peppers,
   sliced into 8 wedges each
1/4 c. shredded Cheddar cheese

Mix cream cheese and olives together in a small bowl. Spread about
2 teaspoons of mixture on each pepper wedge; sprinkle with cheese.
Arrange peppers on an aluminum foil-lined baking sheet. Broil for 6 to
8 minutes, until cheese is melted and peppers begin to char slightly.
Serve warm or cold.

For an elegant yet quick last-minute appetizer, toss a drained jar of Italian antipasto mix with bite-size cubes of mozzarella or provolone cheese. Serve with cocktail picks.

Longhorn Caviar

Makes 3-1/2 cups

1-1/2 c. tomatoes, seeded and
    chopped
16-oz. can black-eyed peas,
    drained
1/3 c. green onions, sliced
2 cloves garlic, minced
3 T. green chiles, diced
2 T. white vinegar
1-1/2 T. fresh cilantro, chopped

1 T. jalapeño pepper, seeded
    and minced
2 t. olive oil
1/4 t. ground cumin
1/4 t. garlic salt
1/8 t. pepper
Garnish: jalapeño slices, fresh
    cilantro sprigs
tortilla chips

In a large bowl, combine all ingredients except garnish and tortilla chips;
cover and chill. Garnish at serving time; serve with tortilla chips.

Garnish summer beverages with fruit-flavored ice cubes.
Cut favorite fruits like watermelon, cantaloupe, kiwi or
honeydew melon into cubes, purée in a food processor
and freeze in ice cube trays.

Over-Stuffed Mushrooms

Serves 4 to 6

1 lb. mushrooms
3 T. grated Parmesan cheese
1 clove garlic, pressed
1 onion, finely chopped
1 c. dry bread crumbs

1 T. fresh parsley, minced
2 T. butter, melted
salt and pepper to taste
6 T. oil, divided

Remove stems from mushrooms; set aside. In a bowl, mix remaining ingredients except oil; spoon into mushroom caps. Spread 2 tablespoons oil in a 13"x9" baking pan; arrange mushrooms in pan. Drizzle remaining oil evenly over mushrooms; bake at 350 degrees for 20 minutes. Serve warm.

Give garlic bread a Greek twist...brush bread slices with
olive oil, sprinkle with lemon-pepper, oregano and garlic.
Top with feta cheese and sliced Kalamata olives. Delicious!

Kit's Herbed Bread

Makes 8 servings

6 T. butter, softened
2 T. fresh parsley, minced
2 green onions, finely chopped
2 t. fresh basil, minced

1 clove garlic, minced
1/4 t. pepper
1 loaf French bread, halved
    lengthwise

Combine all ingredients except bread in a small bowl; mix well. Place bread on an ungreased baking sheet, cut-side up. Spread butter mixture over bread. Broil, 4 inches from heat, for 2 to 3 minutes, or until golden. Slice; serve warm. May be kept refrigerated for up to 2 weeks, or wrap and freeze for one month.

Here's how to tell when rising dough has doubled in size. Press two fingertips into the dough, about 1/2-inch deep, and then release. If the dent remains, the dough has doubled.

Honey-Wheat Bread

Makes 2 loaves

2-1/2 c. warm water, divided
1 T. active dry yeast
1/2 c. honey, divided
1/3 c. olive oil
6 c. whole-wheat flour, divided
1 t. salt

Heat 1/2 cup water until very warm, 110 to 115 degrees. In a small bowl, combine yeast, 1/4 cup honey and 1/2 cup water; set aside for 5 minutes. In a large bowl, mix remaining water, remaining honey, oil, 3 cups flour and salt; add yeast mixture. Stir in remaining flour. Knead dough on a lightly floured surface for 10 minutes. Place dough in a large greased bowl; cover with a tea towel and let rise for 1-1/2 hours, or until double in bulk; punch down. Separate dough into 2 equal portions; shape into loaves. Place in 2 greased 9"x5" loaf pans; cover and let rise 45 additional minutes. Bake at 350 degrees for 30 minutes, or until golden. Remove to cool on wire racks; let cool 20 minutes before slicing.

Don't just think breakfast...use leftover veggies
to make savory dinnertime omelets. Fill omelets with
sautéed vegetables and shredded cheese...scrumptious!
Add a basket of multi-grain English muffins and
dinner is served.

Festive Brunch Frittata

Serves 6

8 eggs
1/2 t. salt
1/8 t. pepper
1/2 c. shredded Cheddar cheese

2 T. butter
2 c. red, green and/or yellow
   peppers, chopped
1/4 c. onion, chopped

Whisk together eggs, salt and pepper. Fold in cheese and set aside. Melt butter over medium heat in an oven-safe non-stick skillet. Add peppers and onion to skillet; sauté until tender. Pour eggs over peppers and onion; do not stir. Cover and cook over medium-low heat for about 9 minutes. Eggs are set when frittata is lightly golden on the underside. Turn oven on broil. Move skillet from stovetop to oven; broil about 5 inches from heat, until top is lightly golden.

Whip up some fruit smoothies for a healthy treat...
delectable made with summer-ripe berries! In a blender,
combine 2 cups of fruit with a cup of vanilla yogurt,
a cup of ice cubes and a tablespoon of honey.
Blend until smooth, pour into tall glasses and enjoy.

Fresh Asparagus Omelet

Serves 2 to 4

1 T. butter
1 T. olive oil
8 stalks asparagus, cut into
    1/2-inch pieces
1/4 onion, chopped

6 eggs, beaten
1/4 c. milk
salt and pepper to taste
1/2 c. shredded Swiss cheese

In a non-stick skillet, heat butter and oil over medium heat. Add asparagus and onion; cook for 5 minutes, or until tender. In a bowl, combine eggs, milk, salt and pepper. Beat egg mixture with a fork just until bubbles begin to appear; pour over asparagus mixture. Cook until eggs set on top; lift edges with a spatula to allow uncooked eggs to run under cooked eggs. When eggs are set, top with cheese. Cut into wedges.

Sew up a quick shopping tote with snips of vintage fabrics like barkcloth and farmhouse calicos. It'll be so handy for carrying home goodies from the farmers' market!

Overnight Maple & Fruit Oatmeal

Serves 8

2 c. milk
1/4 c. maple syrup
1 T. butter, sliced
1 c. long-cooking oats, uncooked
1/2 c. raisins

1 c. apple, peeled, cored and
  chopped
1/2 c. chopped walnuts or pecans
1/2 t. cinnamon
1/8 t. salt

The night before, combine all ingredients in a slow cooker and mix
well. Cover and cook on low setting overnight for 8 to 9 hours. Stir
before serving.

To speed bananas ripening, place them in a plastic bag.
Once they ripen, refrigerate them. The peels will darken,
but the bananas will last for about 2 weeks.

Honey-Baked Bananas

Serves 6

6 bananas, halved lengthwise   1/4 c. honey
2 T. butter, melted   2 T. lemon juice

Arrange bananas in an ungreased 13"x9" baking pan. Blend remaining ingredients; brush over bananas. Bake, uncovered, at 350 degrees for about 15 minutes, turning occasionally. Serve warm.

Want to lighten up a favorite brownie recipe? Replace
some or all of the oil with applesauce or canned pumpkin...
it makes brownies extra moist and works just as well as oil.

Fabulous Zucchini Brownies   *Makes about 1-1/2 dozen*

1-1/2 c. sugar
1/2 c. oil
2 t. vanilla extract
2 c. all-purpose flour
1/2 c. baking cocoa

1 t. baking soda
1 t. salt
2 c. zucchini, shredded
1/2 c. chopped pecans

In a bowl, mix sugar, oil and vanilla; set aside. In a separate bowl, whisk together flour, cocoa, baking soda and salt. Blend in sugar mixture, zucchini and nuts. Pour into a lightly greased 13"x9" baking pan. Bake at 350 degrees for 25 to 30 minutes. Cut into squares.

Plump your raisins for extra flavor before adding them
to a dessert recipe. Simply place the raisins in a bowl
and cover with boiling water. Soak for 15 minutes,
drain and pat dry using a paper towel.

World's Best Carrot Cake

Serves 10

2 c. sugar
2 c. all-purpose flour
1 t. salt
2 t. cinnamon
2 t. baking soda

5 eggs
1-1/2 c. oil
2 c. carrots, peeled and grated
1/2 c. golden raisins

Mix sugar, flour, salt, cinnamon and baking soda in a bowl; set aside. Beat eggs and oil together in a separate bowl; add to dry ingredients. Stir in carrots and raisins; pour into a greased 13"x9" baking pan. Bake at 350 degrees for 30 to 35 minutes, until cake tests done with a toothpick. Cool; spread with icing.

Cream Cheese-Walnut Icing:

8-oz. pkg. cream cheese, softened
1 to 2 T. butter
16-oz. pkg. powdered sugar

1 t. vanilla extract
1 c. chopped walnuts

Blend together cream cheese and butter; add powdered sugar and vanilla. Mix until smooth and creamy; stir in nuts.

For a refreshing summertime treat, top melon wedges
with a scoop of ice cream or sherbet...yummy!

Peanut Butter Power Squares

Makes one dozen

1/2 c. honey
1/2 c. brown sugar, packed
1 c. crunchy peanut butter

4 c. whole-grain rice flake cereal
1 c. dried fruit bits

Bring honey and brown sugar to a boil in a large heavy saucepan over medium-low heat; remove from heat. Mix in peanut butter; stir until melted. Fold in cereal and fruit bits; press mixture into an ungreased 11"x9" baking pan. Cut into squares with a pizza cutter while still warm; cool.

For a quick & easy treat that everybody loves, nothing beats a big bowl of fresh-popped popcorn! Good for you too, because it's a whole grain. To add new flavor, sprinkle on cinnamon-sugar or grated Parmesan cheese.

Powerballs

Makes about 3-1/2 dozen

1 c. creamy peanut butter
1 c. honey
3 c. long-cooking oats, uncooked
1/2 c. ground flaxseed
1 c. semi-sweet chocolate chips

1/2 c. dry-roasted peanuts,
   coarsely chopped
1/4 c. raisins
1/4 c. sweetened dried cranberries

In a large bowl, mix together peanut butter and honey until smooth.
Gradually add oats and flaxseed; mix well. Fold in chocolate chips,
peanuts and dried fruit; blend together gently. Roll into one-inch balls
and place on lightly greased baking sheets. Cover and refrigerate
overnight.

INDEX

INDEX

Our Story

Back in 1984, we were next-door neighbors raising our families in the little town of Delaware, Ohio. Two moms with small children, we were looking for a way to do what we loved and stay home with the kids too. We had always shared a love of home cooking and making memories with family & friends and so, after many a conversation over the backyard fence, **Gooseberry Patch** was born.

We put together our first catalog at our kitchen tables, enlisting the help of our loved ones wherever we could. From that very first mailing, we found an immediate connection with many of our customers and it wasn't long before we began receiving letters, photos and recipes from these new friends. In 1992, we put together our very first cookbook, compiled from hundreds of these recipes and, the rest, as they say, is history.

Hard to believe it's been over 35 years since those kitchen-table days! From that original little **Gooseberry Patch** family, we've grown to include an amazing group of creative folks who love cooking, decorating and creating as much as we do. Today, we're best known for our homestyle, family-friendly cookbooks, now recognized as national bestsellers.

One thing's for sure, we couldn't have done it without our friends all across the country. Each year, we're honored to turn thousands of your recipes into our collectible cookbooks. Our hope is that each book captures the stories and heart of all of you who have shared with us. Whether you've been with us since the beginning or are just discovering us, welcome to the **Gooseberry Patch** family!

Jo Ann & Vickie

Visit our website anytime
www.gooseberrypatch.com

EmailBlogYou Tube

1·800·854·6673